Amish Kinder Komforts

Quilts from the Sara Miller Collection

Written by Bettina Havig

D1404148

American Quilter's Society

P. O. Box 3290 • Paducah, KY 42002-3290

Dedication

To:

My late mother, Susan Schlabach Miller, who instilled in me a deep appreciation of the work and love in these quilts;

Marilyn Woodin, a long-time friend and dealer in quilts, whose interest in quilts inspired me to collect quilts which reflect my Amish heritage;

Steve Evans, a dealer and friend who has helped gather the collection;

Bettina Havig for encouragement and friendship;

And to all the quiltmakers whose timeless quilts enrich my life.

Sara Miller, Kalona, Iowa

To:

Sara Miller for whom I have the greatest respect and love, whose example of patience and generosity temper my days;

My husband, Alan, and daughter Kirsten, whose tolerance of "quilt trotting" allows me to follow the quilts;

And the many anonymous Amish wives and mothers who focused their lives on the child and family and took the time to make a thing of beauty to celebrate childhood.

Bettina Havig, Columbia, Missouri

Located in Paducah, Kentucky, the American Quilter's Society (AQS), is dedicated to promoting the accomplishments of today's quilters. Through its publications and events, AQS strives to honor today's quiltmakers and their work – and inspire future creativity and innovation and innovation in quiltmaking.

Additional copies of this book may be ordered from:

American Quilter's Society
P.O. Box 3290
Paducah, KY 42002-3290
@14.95 Add $2.00 for postage and handling.

Printed in the U.S.A. by Image Graphics

Contents

On the Cover:

Plate 1

Ohio Star

36" x 43", cotton.

The Ohio Star blocks contain an amazing variety of fabrics and value placement, the stars are arranged in clusters like a Nine-Patch.

The quilts have been gathered over the past several years by Sara Miller of Kalona, Iowa. Kalona is the oldest Amish/Mennonite community west of the Mississippi. It was established in the early twentieth century and remains one of the largest concentrations of those church groups. Sara was born in Indiana into a traditional Old Order Amish home. She moved to Kalona with her family as a teenage girl and though she was Amish she had no early interest in the quilts of the Amish. In recent years, as both shop owner and quilt collector, she has become more appreciative of the quilts that she so much took for granted in her youth. Something spurred the interest in Amish quilts and most particularly in crib quilts and other quilts made for or by children.

Very few of the quilts have well established provenance nor can one be established. Quilts made for children are more often consumed by the using and do not survive to become part of a collection of this sort. To find so many and in such variety in one collection is a rare treat. The doll quilts are most probably made by children which helps to explain why they are somewhat crude and primitive. What better way to start instilling the skills needed for quiltmaking than by making it a part of their play. No time or materials are deliberately wasted in an Amish home and even children learn this early.

The construction of the quilts as with Amish quilts in general is by machine. That is to say by treadle machine, an essential item in any Amish home. In many cases the quilting has been done by hand. In a few cases, especially the very small quilts the quilting has been done by machine. Machine quilting is difficult enough to accomplish on a standard home machine and even more so on a treadle machine where so much weight and bulk would have to be controlled while operating the treadle. The quilting is quite simple on all of these quilts. Less elaborate designs have been employed than might be expected on traditional full-sized quilts of the Amish.

The Amish are very family and child centered so it is not surprising that quilts were made for their children. There is no way to project the relative number of crib quilts compared to full-size quilts but the size of Amish families in the first half of the twentieth century would suggest that many might have been needed at one time. All of the quilts included in the collection were made prior to 1950. None appear to be earlier than 1900. They are predominately cotton, reflecting the need to able to wash them frequently. They contain cotton batts or in some cases cotton flannel sheet blankets in place of batts. The palette is much the same as quilts made for use on larger beds. The patterns reflect the patterns common in Amish quilts in general. This collection is a microcosm of quilts of the Amish. It includes the predictable patterns, colors, and styles but also presents the freedom and flexibility of their quilts. A crib quilt offers a small project that might have provided an opportunity to experiment just a little. Today a quiltmaker often might choose such a size to design a wallhanging or other decorative piece. Such whimsy was not likely an option for an Amish quiltmaker. Hopefully you will enjoy the quilts as much as Sara has enjoyed collecting and sharing them.

Plate 2

Nine-Patch Bars

Indiana, 38" x 47", cotton.

It is unusual to see bars oriented on the shorter dimension.

Plate 3

Railroad Crossing variation

39½" x 39½", wool.

Other quilts in the collection have a pieced field and solid crossing, this has a solid field and pieced crossing.

Plate 4

Grape Basket

Illinois, 38½" x 49",
cotton.

Note the irregular strips
in the inner border.

Plate 5

Plain Quilt

Dena Gingerich, Formerly
Oelwein, Iowa, currently,
Clark, Missouri, 34" x 38",
cotton.

Plate 6

Plain Quilt / Center Square

Mrs. Menno Schlabach,
Wayne County, Ohio, 29" x 34",
cotton.

Plate 7

Six Point Star
(or Texas Star)

Oelwein, Iowa, 30" x 40", cotton.

A less common star pattern –
such short seams and tedious
machine construction.

Plate 8

Tumbling Blocks

Ohio, 40" x 53", wool.

Plate 9

34" x 45", wool.

Nothing is known about
this quilt, not even a
name for the pattern if
one exists.

Plate 10

Star Set Nine-Patch

Missouri, 22½" x 33¼".

The setting strips create
the illusion of a star
even though there is no
star block.

Plate 11

Fragmented Bars

Ohio, 32" x 40", cotton.

Plate 12

Double frame plain quilt

Wayne County, Ohio,
32" x 35", cotton.

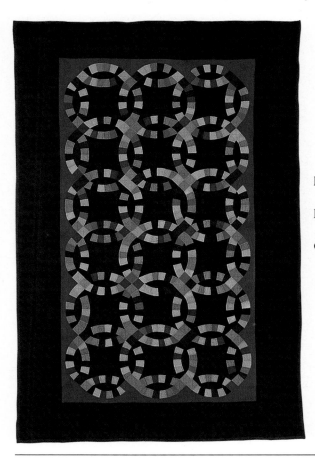

Plate 13

Double Wedding Ring

Ohio, 49" x 73", cotton.

Plate 14

Bull's Eye Log Cabin

35" x 42½", wool and cotton.

Plate 15

Bars

32" x 46", wool and cotton.

A curious quilt, perhaps the practical solution to the cranberry fabrics limited length.

Plate 16

Framed Squares

Ohio, 34½" x 51",
wool.

Plate 17

Spider Star
(or String Star)

34" x 41", cotton.

Plate 18

Amish Log Cabin

33" x 42", cotton.

Plate 19

Skew Log Cabin

Kansas, 28½" x 38", cotton.

Made of irregular uneven width strips squared to fit into the quilt.

Plate 21

Squares

Mrs. Jake Schlabach,
32" x 34", cotton.

Plate 21

Chinese Coins

33½" x 45½", cotton.

Randomly placed color
strips are used to make
vertical bars which
alternate with the solid
bars.

Plate 22

Framed Squares

East central Iowa, 46" x 71", wool.

It is constructed similarly to basic Nine-Patch but with eight squares of one color framing a second color center.

Plate 23

Zigzag

43" x 50", wool.

All constructed of triangles.

Plate 24

Crazy Patch

Illinois or Ohio, 35" x 46½", wool.

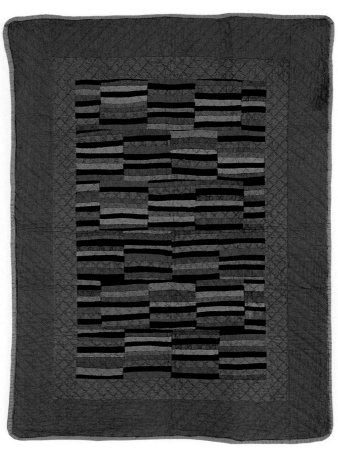

Plate 25

Strip Quilt

Ohio, 29" x 39½", cotton.

Close examination reveals block units are used to create what appears to be random.

Plate 26

Bow Tie

38" x 54", cotton.

Arrangement of blocks makes this quilt reminiscent of an ancient tile floor.

Plate 27

Ocean Waves

Found in Illinois, made in Ohio, 36½" x 47½", cotton.

It has a complicated inner pieced border, unusual for Amish quilts.

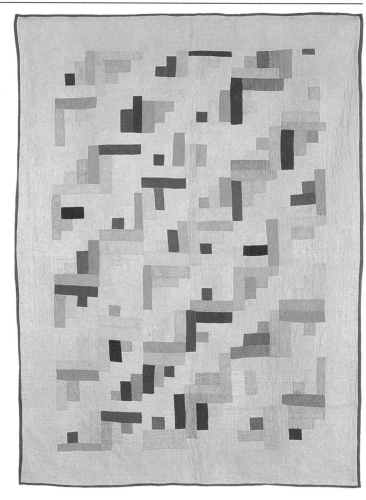

Plate 28

Amish Log Cabin

39½" x 56", cotton.

A very soft subtle palette.

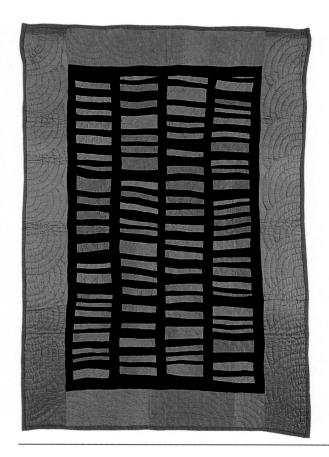

Plate 29

Random Blue Bars

Clark, Missouri, 32" x 46", cotton.

Plate 30

Broken Dishes

Northern Indiana, 34" x 38", cotton.

A unifying navy blue floats the design element of the block.

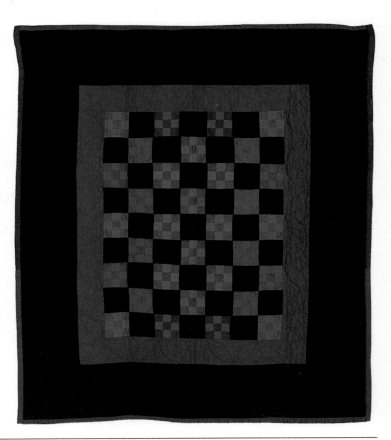

Plate 31

Nine-Patch

Mrs. Joe Gingerich, Wayne County, Ohio, c.1940, 34½" x 40", cotton.

Organized placement of color yields the desired result.

Plate 32

Sunburst

Illinois, 31" x 41", cotton.

Amish quilts often stick to simple block design, this is a notable departure to more complex block.

Plate 33

Double Irish Chain

Wisconsin, 37" x 51½", cotton.

A classic graphic and popular with the Amish.

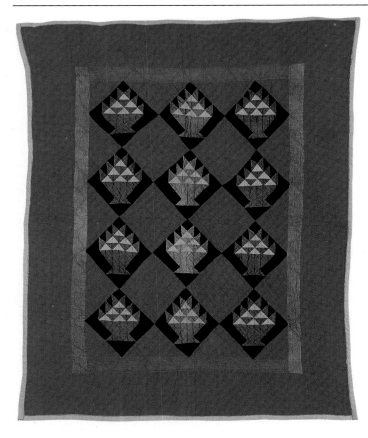

Plate 34

Grape Basket

Mrs. Bontrager, Kansas,
30" x 37½", cotton.

A classic Amish quilt
scaled down to crib size.

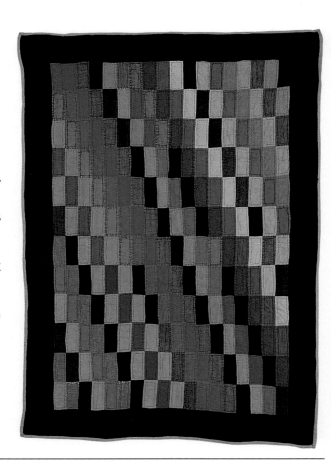

Plate 35 and 37

Bricks

Made by sisters in Oelwein,
Iowa, 34" x 46" and 33" x
46" respectively, cotton.

The quilts differ only in the
choice of framing border.

Plate 36

Made by Mrs. Valentine
Shelter, Ohio, 27" x 38",
cotton.

Randomly positioned
bars and triangles.

Plate 37

Plate 38

Sawtooth Star

Found in Kansas, made in Ohio, 41" x 53", cotton.

Wonderful experimentation with color and value distribution.

Plate 39

Sawtooth Star

Buchanan, Iowa, 28½" x 36½", cotton.

Plate 40

Railroad Crossing, a
variation on the theme

42" x 73", cotton.

Plate 41

Four Baskets

Illinois, 34" x 34", wool.

The strong red is
enhanced by the neutral
black and gray.

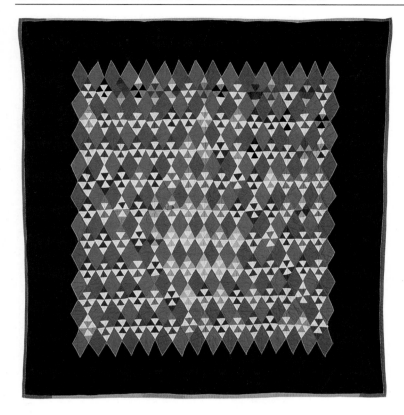

Plate 42

Diamond

Bontrager family,
Kansas, 40" x 43½",
cotton.

The pieced section is
machine appliquéd to
the border frame.

Plate 43

Lone Star (or Star of
Bethlehem)

31" x 41", cotton.

Plate 44

Sunshine and Shadow

Oelwein, Iowa, 37" x 46", cotton.

Has an unusual triple border.

Plate 45

Basket

36" x 42", cotton.

Plate 46

Bear's Paw

Ohio, 35" x 44", cotton.

Note that the four corner blocks are like each other but unlike the remaining Bear's Paw blocks.

Plate 47

Nine-Patch On Point

Illinois, 33" x 40", wool.

A wool quilt in a classic rendering of only 12 simple pieced blocks.

Plate 48

Triangles

Ohio, 46" x 70", cotton.

The quilt is organized in concentric rectangular arrays of triangles.

Plate 49

Evening Star Variations

Kansas, 40" x 45½", cotton.

Here the distribution of values creates very different effects from the same pattern.

Plate 50

Rail Fence –
checkerboard border

34½" x 44", cotton.

Plate 51

Hen and Chickens

34" x 36", cotton.

Strong color within the
blocks actually fool the
viewer about the
boundaries of the block.

Doll Quilts

Plate 52

Rainbow Star (has a companion doll quilt)

Mrs. Menno Mast, Indiana, 31" x 37", cotton.

There are no two star points within the same star of the same color, a very unusual approach to this sort of star.

Plate 53

Nine-Patch

16" x 22", cotton.

Plate 54

Rainbow Star

16" x 19", cotton.

Companion to the Rainbow Star crib quilt in the collection. (Plate #52)

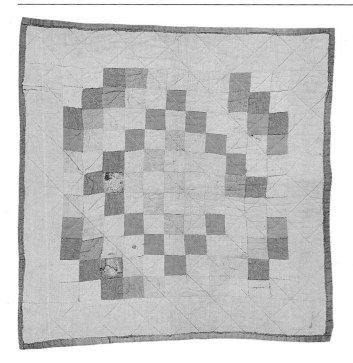

Plate 55

Sunshine and Shadow

16" x 17½", cotton.

Shows use and many launderings –
played with by I wonder how many
children.

Plate 56

Nine-Patch

Kansas, 14" x 17", cotton.

Appears to have three borders but
the third is actually the bound edge.
Amish quilts generally have wide
bindings and in this quilts the scale
creates the illusion of a third border.

Plate 57

Nine-Patch

Leon, Iowa. 16½" x 24", cotton.

Relatively crude construction –
probably a learning piece.

First, you, the quiltmaker may select any colors you want for the quilts. The color suggestions given reflect the colors used in the original quilt in Sara's collection. They are not the only colors suitable for the quilt. Whenever possible, the color of the reverse side, i.e. the lining or backing is indicated so that a complete image of the quilt is rendered.

The Amish have not traditionally employed speed techniques. For the most part they do not use rotary cutters to cut pieces nor do they use strip-piecing techniques. The tools are basic and the results are classic. The directions presented reflect the techniques of the Amish quiltmaker. Sometimes templates are given and sometimes only the measurement of the piece to be cut. When templates are given they will include seam allowances. When cut size is given it too will include seam allowances.

Amish quiltmakers piece by machine albeit a treadle machine. They use up fabric at hand. Often rotary cutting does not hasten the work along when one is cutting small left-over scraps. The method of cutting is left to the discretion of the quiltmaker.

All yardage requirements are for 44" – 45" side fabric.

There are no quilting designs given. The motifs most common to Amish

quilts are also common on these quilts. However the quilting tends to be somewhat less elaborate on these crib quilts than it might be on a full-size quilt. Cables, feathers, and straight line grids are popular with Amish quiltmakers. They infrequently quilt by the piece but don't rule it out. The color of quilting thread may be white, black, or any hue desired. The choice often mirrors the color of the back of the quilt if a basic neutral is not selected.

The size of the quilt in the collection may vary slightly from the size indicated in the pattern and instructions. The size indicated on the pattern reflects adjustments which will make the construction easier. Before cutting long strips which are to be used for borders or setting strips it is wise to measure the actual top or blocks as you work. Variation in seam allowances may effect the dimensions of the top.

Always press the quilt top in preparation for quilting. Press the seams toward the darker fabrics if practical. Press border seams toward the outside edge of the quilt.

Please refer to the appropriate color plate to see the quilt color and value suggestions.

You may wish to photocopy the illustration of a quilt and color it with possible color options before beginning a quilt.

Little Babes, Little Quilts

by Sara Miller

The room is hushed, a baby cries
The little one needs covers,
So underneath the quilt
As the mother gently hovers.

She's taken scraps and has created
A very special piece for her child
Whether wool or cotton, big or small
Some dark colors, some wild.

What did these mothers have in mind
The quiet, gentle ones of the land,
No formal education in art
But some are very well planned.

Others look very contemporary
Also some primitive as you can see
Did they have any idea
Their worth that would come to be?

I must admit, I thought them ugly
So dark and not appealing
But I matured and today, it's true
I love them, it's quite revealing!

Thank you, Lord that I can share
These little quilts from the past
Thank you too, for my rich heritage
The memories of these women will last!

Nine-Patch Bars

39¼" x 48¾"
See Plate 2

This quilt is a variation of the very traditional Bars quilt. Here a Nine-Patch block is turned on point, framed, and five blocks are assembled into a strip or bar. Fifteen Nine-Patch blocks are needed to complete the pieced bars.

Fabric requirements:

½ yd. black
½ yd. royal blue
¾ yd. mauve or lavender
⅜ yd. plum or navy for inner border
¾ yd. royal or cadet blue for outer border
¼ yd. pale blue-gray for binding
1½ yd. wine-claret red for backing
42" x 52" batting – preferably a low loft

The blue used in the blocks may be the same blue as used for the outer border. With Amish quilts you might often see a slight variation in color or dye lot depending on available fabrics, i.e. scraps on hand versus new purchases made to complete the project.

Templates: Finished block size is 4¼".

Template A: cut 60 black, 75 blue
Template B: cut 60 mauve

Or rotary cut squares for Nine-Patch; cut each square 1⅝" x 1⅝", four black and five blue for each Nine-Patch. A total of 60 black and 75 blue. To rotary cut for B, cut 30 squares 3¼" x 3¼", cut squares in half on the diagonal (60 triangles).

Construction:

Each Nine-Patch block consists of four black and five blue squares.

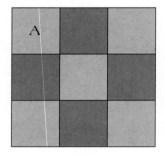

fig. 1

The block is completed by adding a triangle, B, to the four corners of the Nine-Patch block, press seams to outer corners.

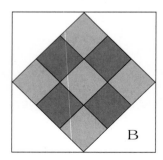

fig. 2

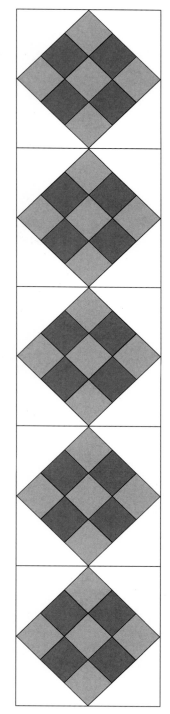

fig. 3

Cut four strips of black 5¼" x 24¼" each.
Stitch five blocks in a strip or bar.
Alternate pieced bar and plain bar, four plain and three pieced to complete the center of the top. Press seams toward plain bars.

For inner border: cut two strips 2¾" x 33¼" and two strips 2¾" x 28¾".

For outer border: cut two strips 5¾" x 39¼" and two strips 5¾" x 38¼".

Cut four binding strips, each 2" wide across the width of the fabric.

A quilting note – Blocks: in diagonal lines across the patches, inner border: wine glass or tea cup in inner border, outer border: double angled lines, plain bars: fat cable.

Templates for Nine-Patch Bars

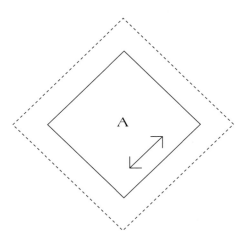

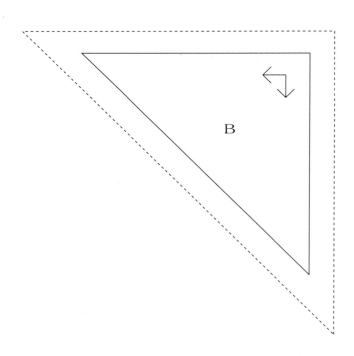

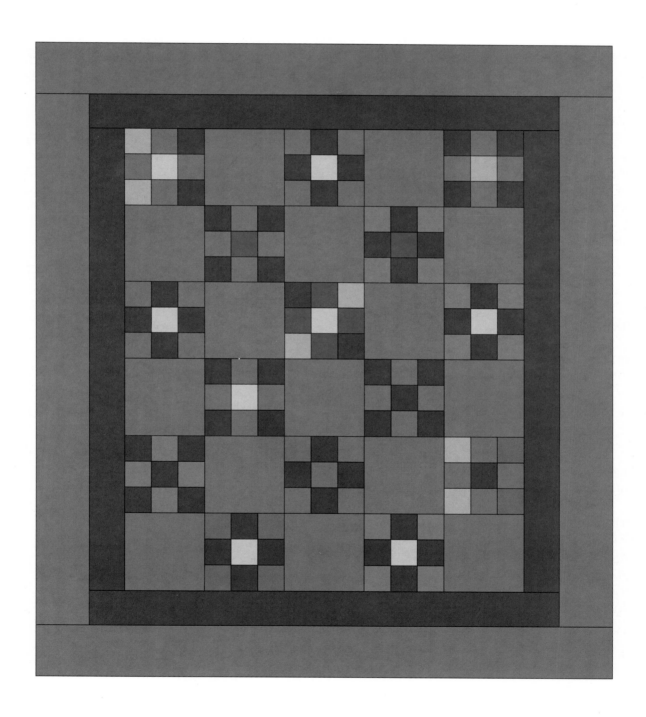

Nine-Patch Doll Quilt

16¼" x 39½"
See Plate 56

Nothing makes a more charming wallhanging than a doll quilt. Probably used to help teach a girl to piece, this little quilt reflects the work of a novice but the workmanship does not detract from its charm.

Fabric requirements:

⅛ yd. each of 6 – 8 colors (equal distribution of light and dark values) or enough scraps to cut at least 144 assorted 1¼" squares
⅜ yd. slate blue-gray
½ yd. black for inner border and backing
18" x 21" batting

Template: Finished block size is 2¼".

template A template B

Cutting:

Rotary cutting squares this small and in this variety may be more hassle than its worth – you decide.

For the Nine-Patch blocks:
Cut 144 squares from template A in assorted colors, equally divided between light and dark.
Or rotary cut 144 – 1¼" squares in assortment as above. For setting block cut 20 – 2¾" squares of slate blue-gray.

Construction:

Piece 15 Nine-Patch blocks (fig. 1).

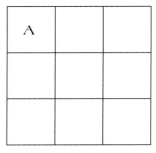

fig. 1

Assembling the quilt:

Assemble the quilt in 6 rows. Rows 1, 3, and 5 alternate three Nine-Patch with two plain alternate blocks of slate blue-gray; rows 2, 4, and 6 alternate two Nine-Patch blocks with three alternate squares of slate blue-gray (fig. 2 and 3).

Borders:

For black inner border cut two strips 1½" x 14" and two strips 1½" x 13¾". Attach sides first, then top and bottom.

For slate blue-gray outer border cut two strips 2" x 16" and two strips 2" x 16¼".

Binding type I, suggested finished size of ½".

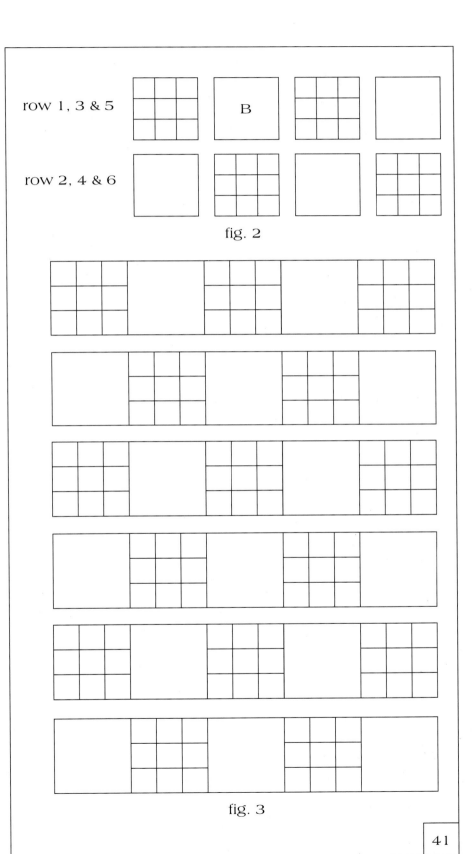

row 1, 3 & 5   B

row 2, 4 & 6

fig. 2

fig. 3

Templates for Nine-Patch Doll Quilt

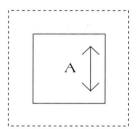

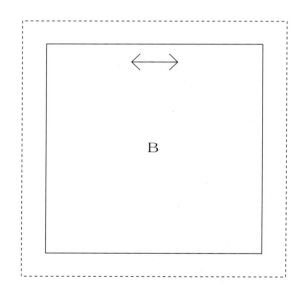

Plain Quilt / Center Square

29" x 34"
See Plate 6

No group of Amish quilts would be complete without a plain quilt, that is a quilt with no pieced block design. The quilting on this quilt is quite simple. On a full-size Amish quilt of this type the quilting would take center stage and become a major factor in the design of the quilt. Because this is a child's quilt perhaps the maker felt that the intense quilting was not necessary. The real joy of quilting is experienced when working on a blank area like the center of this quilt. There are no seams to interrupt the flow of your stitching.

There are no templates given for this quilt, only measurements. Please be as careful as possible. Cut accurately.

Fabric requirements:

1 yd. navy
1 yd. emerald green
1¼ yd. emerald green – the same or it may a different dye lot or manufacturer
33" x 38" batting

Cutting:

For center panel cut navy 16½" x 21½".

For inner border cut two strips 2" x 21½" and two strips 2" x 20". Attach sides, then top and bottom.

For outer border cut two strips 5½" x 24½" and two strips 5½" x 29". Attach sides, then top and bottom.

The center panel of the quilt is quilted with a simple cross-hatch. The borders have a fan design spanning both borders. These represent perhaps the fastest options for quilting, no doubt a factor in their selection.

The quilt is bound from the back, type I binding. No more than 1" wide is recommended.

STAR SET NINE-PATCH

23¾" x 33¼"
See Plate 10

The real block in this quilt is a simple Nine-Patch but the illusion is that a star block is used. The star appears because of the construction of the set for the quilt and no actual star block is made. The dogtooth bordered edge of the quilt is very rarely done on Amish quilts. It requires appliqué of the long strip cut to create the teeth. Appliqué is not a technique favored by the Amish quiltmaker. Appliqué is not the optimum stewardship of resources. (No directions are given for the dogtooth border.)

Fabric requirements:

1 yd. clear sky blue
1¾ yd. white
¾ yd. lining – white or color of your choice
⅛ yd. blue for separate binding
24" x 36" batting

Templates: Finished block size is 3¾".
A, B, and C

Cutting for blocks:

By template A: cut 60 blue, 75 white
Or rotary cutting: cut 60 blue and 75 white squares each 1¾" x 1¾".

For set: template B cut 38 white, template C cut 152 blue, and template A cut 24 blue

Or rotary cutting: cut 38 white rectangles, 1¾" x 4¼", cut 152 blue squares each 1½" x 1½"; and 24 blue squares 1¾" x 1¾".

Construction of the quilt:

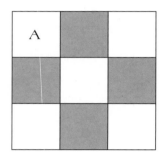

fig. 1

Assemble 15 Nine-Patch blocks.

For the setting units:

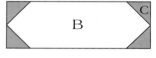

fig.2

By template method: attach a blue triangle to each angle corner of the setting piece B.

By rotary cutting method: attach a blue square to each corner of the setting rectangle stitching on the diagonal of the square.

Trim away the excess at the corners.

fig. 3a

fig. 3b

Assembling the quilt:

Rows 1, 3, 5, 7, 9, and 11 consist of cornerstone square A alternated with setting unit (four cornerstones plus three setting units).

fig. 4

Rows 2, 4, 6, 8, 10 consist of setting units alternating with Nine-Patch block (four setting units plus three Nine-Patch blocks).

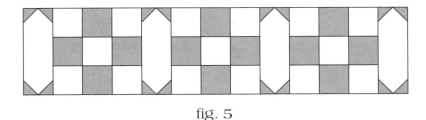

fig. 5

This quilt has only one border, a 3¾" white border framing the center of the quilt. For the border cut strips of white 4" wide. Two strips 4" x 26¾" and two strips 4" x 23¾". Attach side borders first and then top and bottom. Remember to verify actual lengths before cutting your border.

In place of the appliquéd dogtooth border a wide separate blue binding, type II is suggested.

Templates for Star Set Nine-Patch

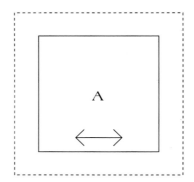

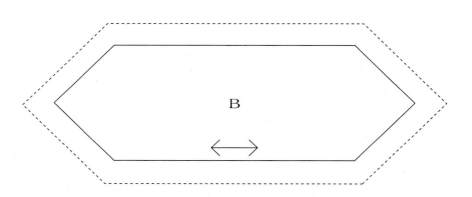

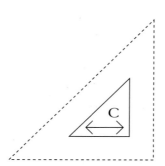

Bull's Eye Log Cabin

35½" x 43¾"
See Plate 14

There are two unusual characteristics of this quilt, first the bull's eye effect and second the use of lattice strips in a Log Cabin style quilt. The end result is extremely graphic and powerful. There is a mix of warm and cool colors in the blocks. The bottle green used to set the quilt is also the choice for the first or inner border of the quilt. The green in the original quilt is wool crepe but you will probably prefer not mixing wool and cotton fabrics in your quilt.

Fabric requirements:

For each block two colors are needed, black and one other. Select vibrant high contrast colors like true red, royal blue, magenta, or bright purple.

¼ yd. each of 3 – 4 colors
1⅜ yd. black includes outer border
¾ yd. bottle green for lattice and inner border
½ yd. lavender or muted purple for separate binding
1½ yd. goldenrod for backing
40" x 48" batting

No templates are given, measure and cut strips with scissors or rotary cutter.
Finished block size is 7".

Cutting:

For each block, cut center square 1½" x 1½" and cut strips across fabric 1¼" wide and then cut to length needed for each log.

In all except one of the blocks the rounds begin with black so #1, 2, 3, and 4, and 9, 10, 11, and 12 are black. #5, 6, 7, and 8, and #13, 14, 15, and 16 are contrast color.

Strips are cut 1¼" wide by the following lengths:

Black
#1: 1½"
#2 and #3: 2¼"
#4: 3"
#9: 4½"
#10 and #11: 5¼"
#12: 6"

Color
#5: 3"
#6 and #7: 3¾"
#8: 4½"
#13: 6"
#14 and #15: 6¾"
#16: 7½"

See fig. 1 for color placement by number.

Construction:

Begin with the center square and add strips in numeric order (fig. 1).

For the lattice cut eight bottle green strips 1¾" wide x 7½" long and three strips 1¾" x 24".

Assembling the quilt: refer to quilt layout diagram.

You will need 12 Log Cabin blocks. Assemble the quilt in horizontal rows consisting of three Log Cabin blocks and two short lattice strips. There will be four rows. Connect the rows with the 24" long lattice strips. The interior of the quilt should measure 24" x 32¼". Verify measurements before cutting border strips.

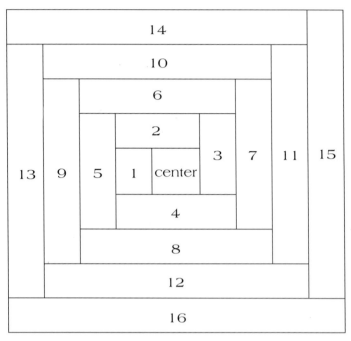

fig. 1

Borders:

For inner border cut two side strips 1 ¾ x 32¼" and cut top and bottom strips 1¾" x 26½". Attach side, then top and bottom.

For outer border cut two side strips 5¼" x 34¾" and cut top and bottom strips 5¼" x 35½". Attach side, then top and bottom

Type II binding, suggested finished width of ¾".

layout

Amish Log Cabin

33" x 41"
See Plate 18

Amish Log Cabin blocks differ slightly from English Log Cabin. There is one less round of fabric so blocks are an even number of strips across. The first square is part of the cabin but not the true center of the block. This method yields a slight difference on the weight of the light and dark sides of the quilt, in an English Log Cabin they are essentially equal but in an Amish Log Cabin they are distinctly not.

Fabric requirements:

¼ yd. black (sateen if you can find it)
⅛ yd. each of 4 – 6 colors including pale blue, soft green, aqua, lavender, mauve
½ yd. flat black for inner border
⅔ yd. deep navy for outer border
1⅜ yd. mauve for backing
39" x 48" batting

No templates given, cut strips to size. Finished block size is 4".

Cutting:

Scissors or rotary cut, if rotary cutting you may want to cut strips of all fabrics 1½" wide and then cut to correct length.

For each block cut: one strip of each size in indicated color – mix the colors, keeping the color side of the block cool:

#1: 1½" x 1½" black
#2: 1½" x 1½" color
#3: 1½" x 2½" color
#4: 1½" x 2½" black
#5: 1½" x 3½" black
#6: 1½" x 3½" color
#7: 1½" x 4½" color

Be sure that you mix the colors, creating a scrappy impression.

Construction:

Piece each Amish Log Cabin block beginning with #1 and adding pieces in order as numbered in fig. 1. Piece 24 blocks.

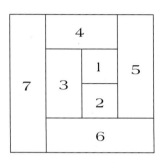

fig. 1

Assembling the quilt:

The arrangement of the blocks in the quilt is referred to as Straight Furrow, creating a diagonal flow of black and color across the quilt (fig. 2).

Borders:

For inner border cut two strips 3½" x 24½" and two strips 3½" x 30½". Attach side borders, then top and bottom.

For outer border cut two strips 6" x 36½" and two strips 6" x 34". Attach side borders, then top and bottom.

The back of the quilt is mauve and is brought over to the top to form a type I self binding (see binding information).

A quilting note – the quilting is an allover crosshatch grid, spaced at about 1".

fig. 2

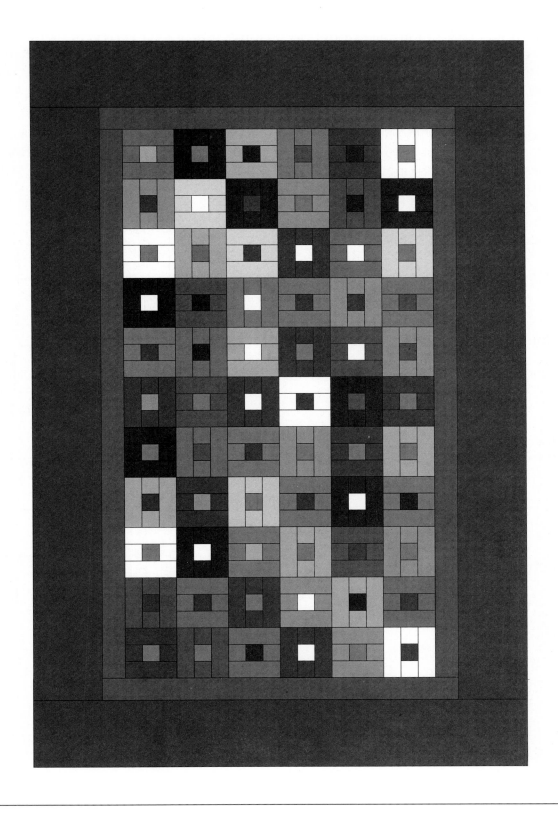

Framed Squares

43" x 65½"
See Plate 22

The framed squares quilt in the collection is a bit large for most cribs but small enough to assume that it was made for a child's use. The size of the quilt has been adjusted for these instructions to simplify construction.

Fabric requirements:

⅛ yd. assorted solid colors, 8 to 10 different, such as goldenrod, burgundy, navy, royal blue, charcoal gray, forest green, dark teal, brown
⅜ yd. dusty teal for inner border
⅞ yd. deep, dark navy for outer border
2 yds. backing, color of your choice
45" x 70" batting

Templates: Finished block size is 4½".

template A and template B

Or rotary cutting: for each block cut two 2" x 5" color 1, and two 2" x 2" color 1, and one 2" x 2" color 2.

Cutting:

For each block select two colors and cut:

A: cut 2 color #1
B: cut 2 color #1
B: cut 1 color #2

You need a total of 66 blocks using a variety of color combinations. Mix the palette.

The block is much like a Nine-Patch but simplified to use only five pieces of fabric per block (fig. 1).

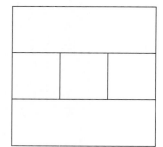

fig. 1

Assembling the quilt:
fig. 2

Assemble the quilt in
11 rows of six blocks.
Turn alternate blocks
which will help con-
trol any drift or distor-
tion.

Borders:

For inner border cut
two strips 2½" x 50"
(verify the length from
the top before cut-
ting), and two strips
2½" x 31½". Attach
sides, then top and
bottom.

For outer border cut
two strips 6½" x 53½"
and two strips 6½" x
43". Attach sides,
then top and bottom.

fig. 2

Templates for Framed Squares

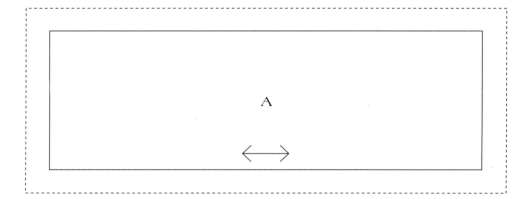

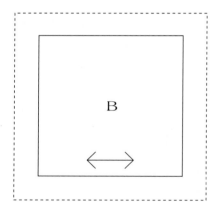

Bow Tie

40" x 56"
See Plate 26

This is one of the relatively rare Amish quilts with only a single border. Each Bow Tie block measures 4" and the field of design is framed with an equal 4" border. There are three colors plus black in the quilt in the collection but instructions are given with only two colors plus black since the third color was probably originally only a different dye lot of the deeper hue. The entire quilt surface is quilted with a cross-hatch totally disregarding the blocks and border spaces.

Fabric requirements:

1 yd. cranberry
1 yd. rose-pink
2¾ yd. black (includes border)
1¾ yd. gray for backing (includes self binding)
42" x 58" batting

Templates: A and B. Finished block size is 4".

Cutting for the entire quilt of 96 Bow Tie blocks:

A: cut 192 black
A: cut 96 cranberry
A: cut 96 rose-pink
B: cut 48 cranberry
B: cut 48 rose-pink

Construction:

fig. 1 and fig. 2

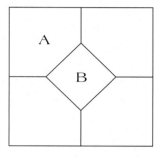

fig. 1

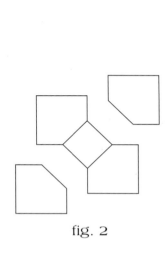

fig. 2

Assembling the quilt:

Lay out rows following the color placement in quilt layout. Final construction is easier if you make eight rows of 12 blocks per row. It means fewer seams to match as you assemble the quilt top.

Verify the dimensions of your top before cutting border strips.

Borders:

Cut two strips 4¼" x 48½" for long sides and two strips 4¼" x 40¼" for shorter sides. Attach border to longer sides first then attach remaining sides.

The quilt is bound from the back (type I). Suggested size, 1¼".

Templates for Bow Tie

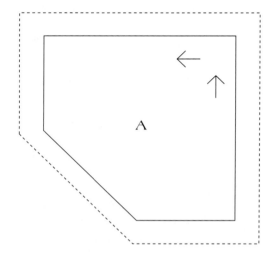

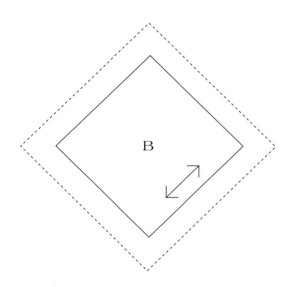

Broken Dishes

33¼" x 37¼"
See Plate 30

Broken Dishes is one of the simplest of all patterns to construct. In this quilt it yields on unusual effect of rows of bows. The visual effect is achieved by carefully placing the colors used for the blocks. The blocks are set with alternate plain blocks in a dark navy which creates a negative space on which the blocks are suspended.

Fabric requirements:

½ yd. rose includes binding
¼ yd. cream
¼ yd. medium blue
1½ yd. navy includes alternate blocks and outer border
½ yd. black includes inner border
1⅛ yd. backing color of your choice
40" x 44" batting

Templates: Finished block size is 3".

Template A for piecing Broken Dishes block and Templates B, C, and D for alternate blocks and set. A, B, C, and D

Cutting:

For each block:
total of 30 blocks needed

A: cut 2 black, 2 navy, and 4 rose, blue, or cream
B: cut 20 navy
C: cut 18 navy
D: cut 4 navy

Or rotary cut:

For triangles A: cut 2⅜" squares and cut in half on diagonal. For alternate block B: cut twenty 3½" squares. To fill triangles on the sides, top and bottom: cut five 1¼" squares and cut in quarters diagonally. For corners cut two 3⅞" squares cut in half on the diagonal.

Construction:

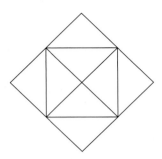

fig. 1

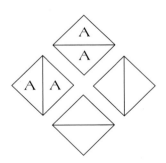

fig. 2

You need 12 rose blocks, 12 blue blocks, six cream blocks.

Assembly:

Assemble the blocks in diagonal rows beginning with a corner. The center portion of the top consisting of 30 pieced blocks plus the setting blocks should measure 21¼" x 25½".

Borders:

For inner border cut two strips for sides 1⅞" x 26" and two strips for top and bottom 1⅞" x 24". Attach sides, then top and bottom.

For outer border cut two side strips 5⅛" x 28¾" and two strips for top and bottom 5⅛" x 33¼". Attach sides, then top and bottom.

The binding is type II. Suggested finished width of 1".

Templates for Broken Dishes

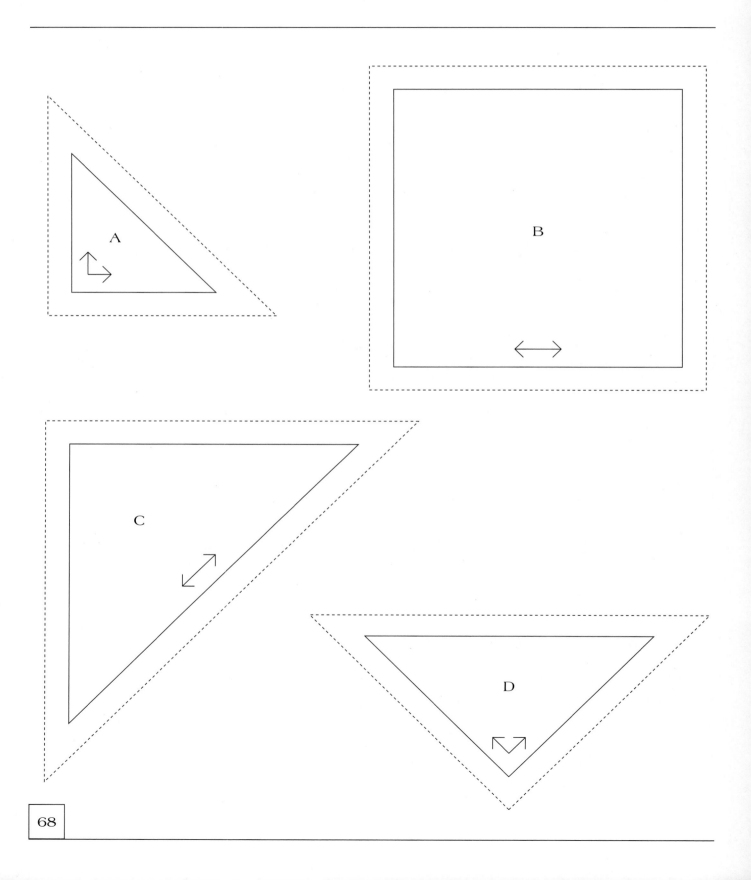

Grape Basket

32½" x 39½"
See Plate 34

Pieced baskets of many variations are popular with Amish quiltmakers. This is one of the more complex variations and uses an unusual fabric, blue chambray.

Fabric requirements:

⅜ yd. black
¼ yd. peach
½ yd. blue chambray (includes inner border)
1 yd. bright maroon or burgundy (includes outer border)
1½ yd. camel, tan, or soft yellow (includes backing and self binding)

Templates: Finished block size 5".

(A, B, C, D, and E for the block)

For each basket block:

A: cut 1 blue chambray
B: cut 2 black
C: cut 1 black
D: cut 1 black
E: cut 6 peach and 11 blue chambray

There are 12 blocks in the quilt.

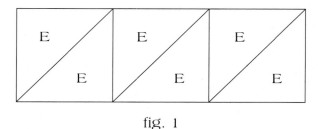

fig. 1

For setting the quilt with alternate unpieced blocks you will need six squares cut 5½" x 5½". For the ten triangles for the side insets, cut three squares 6¾" x 6¾" and divide the squares into four triangles by cutting diagonally in both directions (this leaves two extra triangles). This will keep grain lines of the fabric along the longest side of the triangles. For the corners cut two squares 4⅜" x 4⅜" which will be cut in half on the diagonal yielding the four corner triangles. If all cutting is done correctly you will have grainline on all outside edges. These may be rotary cut.

Construction:

12 basket blocks are needed (fig. 1, 2, and 3).

Assembling the quilt:

Arrange the basket blocks and the alternate blocks and assemble in diagonal rows (fig. 4).

Borders:

For inner blue chambray border cut two strips 1¾" x 28½" for the sides and two strips 1¾" x 24" for the top and bottom. Attach sides first and then top and bottom border strips.

For outer border cut two strips 4¾" x 31" for sides and two strips 4¾" x 32½" for top and bottom. Attach sides first then top and bottom border strips.

Bind from the back. See binding information and chart.

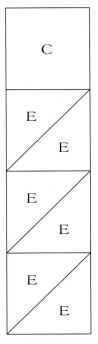

fig. 2

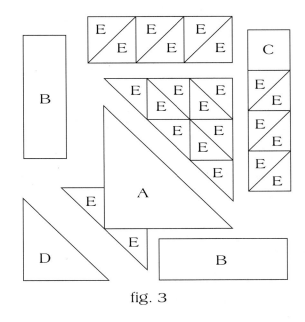

fig. 3

fig. 4

Templates for Grape Basket

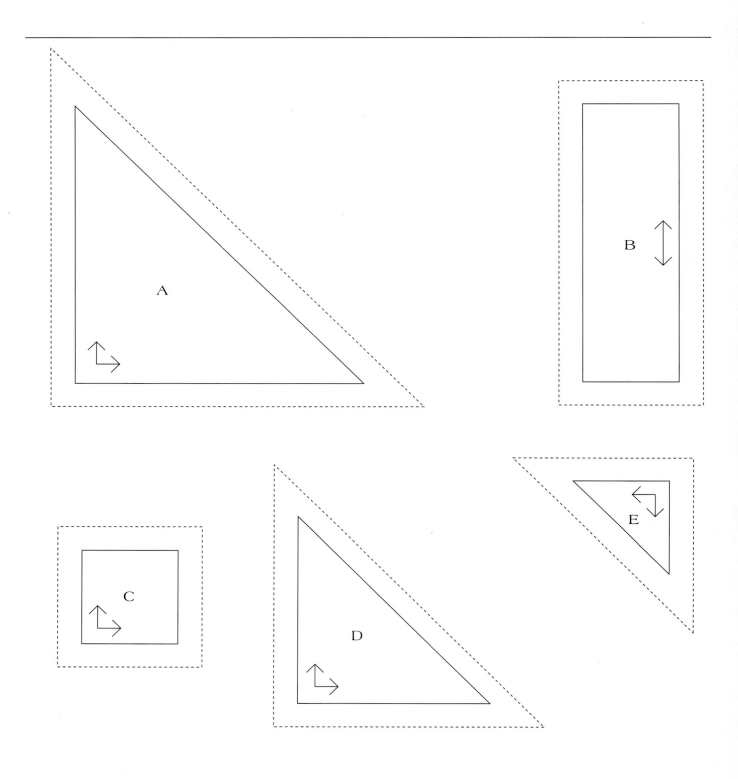

Rainbow Star

30½ x 36
See Plate 52

Unlike most Eight-Pointed Stars which have one or two colors in the star points this star block has eight in each block – each point of the star is a different color. The back of this quilt is flour sacking which may still be available to you if you inquire at your local bakery. The background of each star and the wide outer border of the quilt are white, a color sometimes left out of the Amish palette. There are no colors for which the Amish hold disdain. White is simply harder to keep clean than the darker colors we have come to expect. However white scraps are generated in the production of some garments and therefore do find their way into the quilts. Both this quilt and its companion doll quilt are set block to block with similar inner and outer border.

Fabric requirements:

Assorted scraps of rainbow hues – not too much of any one color – an 8" square of any color is sufficient.

1 yd. white includes background and border
½ yd. royal or cadet blue for inner border and separate binding
1 yd. white for backing (or one large flour sack)
36" x 40" batting

Templates:

A, B, and C for the star block 5½" finished block.

Cutting for the quilt:

A: cut a total of 96 diamonds in a variety of colors, use a color only one point per star.
B: cut 48 white
C: cut 48 white

Piecing the block:

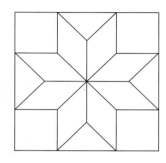

fig. 1

Assembling the quilt:

Assemble four rows of three stars per row. The interior of the quilt should measure 17" x 22½".

Borders:

For the inner border cut side strips 2" x 22½" and cut top and bottom strips 2" x 20". Attach sides, then top and bottom.

For outer border cut side strips 6" x 25½" and cut top and bottom strips 6" x 30½". Attach sides, then top and bottom.

Type II separate binding, finished size ¾".

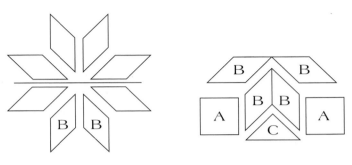

fig.2

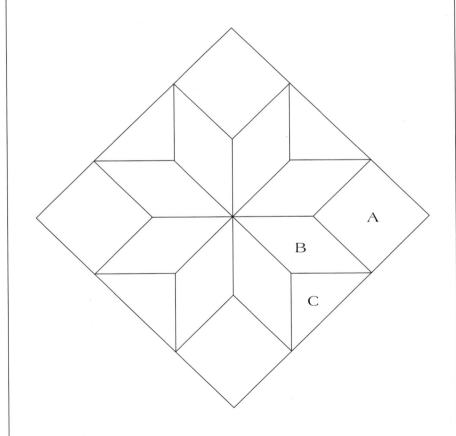

Templates for Rainbow Star

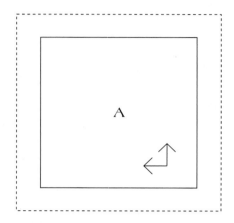

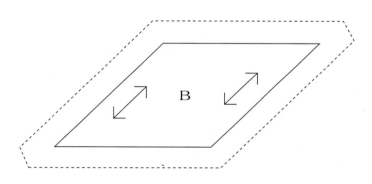

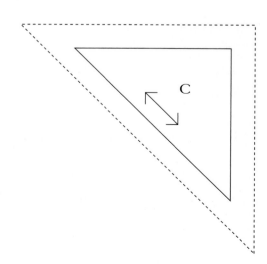

Sawtooth Star

41" x 53"
See Plate 38

Have some fun with this block. The Amish quiltmaker seems to have tried every possible combination and placement of color and value to achieve a myriad of different looks. There are 70 blocks, utilizing at least a dozen colors, randomly distributing the values. Each block measures 3" finished. The quiltmaker who undertook this quilt for a child's use truly made a statement of devotion and love.

Fabric requirements:

⅜ yd. each 12 – 15 different colors and values (or bundles of assorted scraps). There are a lot of sateens in the original quilt, include as many as you can find to try to duplicate the look.
½ yd. royal blue inner border and use some for blocks
1⅜ yd. black for outer border
1¾ yd. black sateen for backing (or flat black)
45" x 57" batting

Templates: Finished block size is 3".

A, B, C, and D

Cutting

For each block:
A: cut 1
B: cut 8
C: cut 4
D: cut 4

Color decisions are up to you, vary the emphasis of the block, distribute the values and watch the blocks emerge.

There are 70 blocks.

For setting:

Cut 60 strips 1½" x 3½" and 9 strips 1½" x 27½".

Construction:

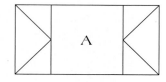

fig. 1

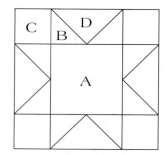

fig. 2

Assembling the quilt:

Assemble the quilt in ten rows of seven blocks per row using lattice strips for connectors. Join the rows with the long strips you have cut.

Hint: mark the long strips and pin the corners of the blocks to align with the blocks of the preceding row.

Verify the lengths before making the final cuts.

Borders:

For inner border cut two strips 2½" x 39" and two strips 2½" x 31½". Attach sides, then top and bottom.

For outer border cut two strips 5½" x 43½" and two strips 5½" x 41". Attach sides, then top and bottom.

Type I binding is suggested, finished size ½".

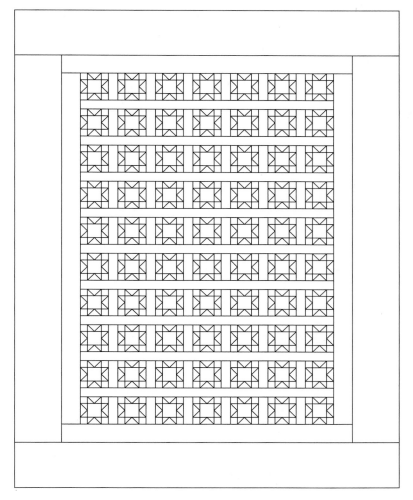

layout

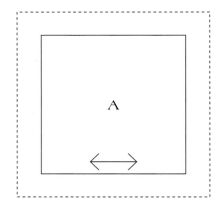

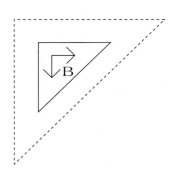

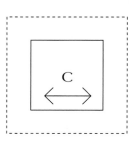

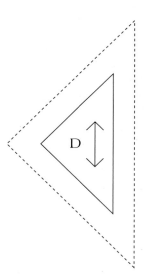

Ohio Star

35⅝" x 42⅜"
See Plate 1

The confetti look of the quilt is obtained by totally abandoning your compulsion to organize the colors for each block. The placement of color appears to be completely random. This cavalier attitude may be difficult for many of us to achieve. Try putting the pieces into a brown bag or other container and pulling them out without looking. "Take whatever comes," a life's attitude for the Amish. If you try to make your quilt too structured and organized you will sacrifice the wonderful feeling of this quilt.

Fabric requirements:

The original quilt is almost entirely made of sateen – something virtually impossible today because the selection of color in sateen is not readily available.

There are at least a dozen different colors, shades and tints present in this quilt.

⅛ yd. each of 12 – 16 colors including blues, grays, cranberry, black, forest green, lavender, and cream
⅛ yd. each of two blues not already used in the piecing
¼ yd. black
¼ yd. cocoa brown (a reddish brown, not too dark)
1 yd. royal blue or navy blue (again choose one not already included)
1½ yds. dark, cool color for backing
40" x 48" batting

Templates: Finished block size is 3⅜".

template A   template B

Cutting:

There are 23 blocks needed for the quilt, each block requires the use of 12 A and 5 B. For the confetti look begin cutting 276 assorted triangles from template B and 115 squares from template A.

Or for rotary cutting:

A equals squares cut 1⅝" x 1⅝"; B equals squares cut 2⅜" x 2⅜" and cut into four triangles by cutting on both diagonals. Cut 115 squares for A and at least 70 squares for B triangles. The more variety the better so be willing to cut extra to allow for greater choice.

Construction:

Piece 23 blocks. The setting arrangement for the blocks is much like a double Nine-Patch. There are five Ohio Star blocks arranged alternately with a plain square to form a section. Refer to the quilt layout for the complete set. The alternate plain blocks are of two shades of blue. Cut the squares 3⅞" x 3⅞". The setting strips are black, cut eight strips 3⅞" x 10⅝".

Assembling the quilt:

Relax and let the blocks come together quite randomly, abandon your inhibitions about color, value, and structure and enjoy the results.

See the diagram of the quilt and assemble the center of the quilt by first completing the Ohio Star Nine-Patch units, you need four. Complete the set.

Borders:

Always verify the lengths before cutting for borders. They should be as follows:

For inner border cut two side strips 1½" x 30⅞" and two strips for top and bottom 1½" x 24⅛". Attach the side borders, then top and bottom.

For outer border cut two side strips 5½" x 32⅞" and two strips for top and bottom 5½" x 35⅝". Attach side, then top and bottom.

Type II binding, finished recommended size ¾".

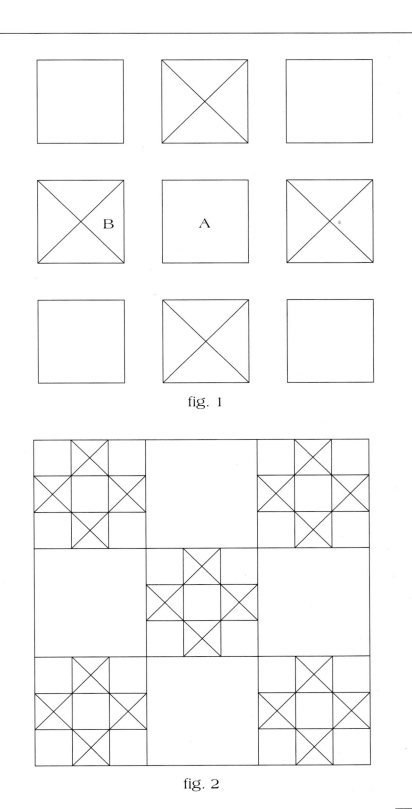

fig. 1

fig. 2

Templates for Ohio Star

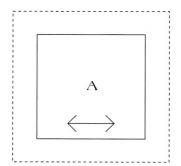

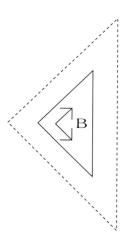

Amish quiltermakers prefer one of two ways to bind their quilts, a self binding from the back or a separate binding cut on straight grain of the fabric. Bias binding especially on quilts of the vintage of Sara's collection is virtually non-existent.

Type I:

A great number of Amish quilts are bound from the backing, a self binding, done by bringing the backing fabric over to the top and stitching it down. It is important to prepare for the type of binding you will use as you plan your quilt. To bind using the self-bound method you must be careful to keep the top and batt well centered on the backing to allow for the margin needed to self bind without wasted fabric. It is also important to complete the quilting before trimming and preparing the quilt for binding regardless of the method chosen. In calculating the size of the backing for type I binding, you should allow a minimum two inch extension on all four sides. For example if the quilt measures 20" x 30" the backing and batting should both be cut at least 24" x 34". This allows for a slightly wider binding than you would expect from a bias binding. For best results follow these steps:

1. Determine the desired width of finished binding. See Chart 1, column 1.

2. Begin trimming with the batting only. Trim the batting leaving a margin of batting determined by Chart 1, column 2.

3. Now trim the backing to the size indicated in Chart 1, column 3.

4. Turn under the outside edge of the backing ¼". Turn down toward the quilt top. Bring the binding margin over to the top of the quilt. Slipstitch in place (Amish quilters would most probably stitch this by machine but you may not want to see these stitches). As you complete one full edge length turn and fold under the raw edges at the end on the side. Do not miter the corners.

Desired width of binding	Batting margin	Backing margin
¼"	0"	½"
⅜"	⅛"	¾"
½"	¼"	1"
⅝"	⅜"	1¼"
¾"	½"	1½"
⅞"	⅝"	1¾"
1"	¾"	2"
1⅛"	⅞"	2¼"

Type II binding:

This is a separate binding applied to the quilt by cutting four strips of specific width, completing each side independently of the others. This type of binding is also very popular with Amish quiltmakers, it satisfies their conservative demands on fabric but it does require long, narrow strips of fabric.

To use type II binding, first determine the desired finished width of the binding. Cut strips of fabric for binding following the information in Chart 2. Always cut the strips at least 1" longer than the length of the side to which it will be sewn. Cut two strips for the length and two strips for the width.

1. After the quilting is completed, trim the batting and backing of the quilt as indicated on Chart 2, column 2.

2. Attach each strip with the right side facing the top of the quilt to the edge of the top; center the strip along the side so that you will have at least ½" extension on each end. Finish each side before beginning the next side of the quilt.

3. Stitch strips through all four layers (strip, top, batting, and backing). Turn to the back of the quilt.

4. Turn the binding over the quilt edge to the back of the quilt; fold under ¼" seam allowance and slipstitch the binding to the back of the quilt. Bring the folded edge all the way to the stitching line from attaching the binding strip to reverse side. Use the extra length on each of the strip to finish the end of each side of binding before going on to the next side.

Note: Keep in mind the overall proportions of the quilt and that the Amish use a binding wider than English style, but don't let the binding overpower the quilt. Be certain that the binding width does not intrude on the quilting designs used on the border. If an overall design is used there is no need worry but if there is a feather, cable, or other separate design, protect its integrity.

Desired width of binding	Trim margin for batting and backing (beyond top)	Cut width of binding
¼"	0"	1"
⅜"	⅛"	1¼"
½"	¼"	1½"
⅝"	⅜"	1¾"
¾"	½"	2"
⅞"	⅝"	2¼"
1"	¾"	2½"
1⅛"	⅞"	2¾"
1¼"	1"	3"
1⅜"	1⅛"	3¼"
1½"	1¼"	

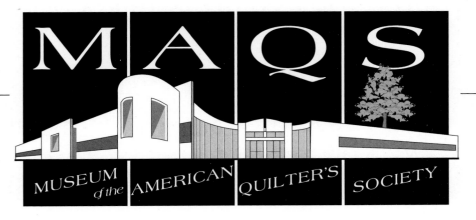

Museum of the American Quilter's Society
215 Jefferson St. / P. O. Box 1540
Paducah, KY 42002-1540
502-442-8856

A dream long held by American Quilter's Society founders Bill and Meredith Shroeder and by quilters worldwide was realized on April 25, 1991, when the Museum of the American Quilters Society (MAQS, pronounced "Max") opened its doors in Paducah Kentucky. As it is stated in brass lettering over the building's entrance, this non-profit institution is dedicated to "honoring today's quilter," by stimulating and supporting the study, appreciation, and development of quiltmaking throughout the world.

The 30,000 square foot facility includes a central exhibition gallery featuring a selection of the 135 quilts by contemporary quiltmakers comprising the museum's permanent collection, and two additional galleries displaying exhibits of antique and contemporary quilts. Lectures, workshops, and other related activities are also held on site, in spacious modern classrooms. A gift and book shop makes available a wide selection of fine crafts and quilt books. The museum is open year-round, Tuesday through Saturday, and is handicapped accessible.

For more information, write:

MAQS
P.O. Box 1540
Paducah, KY 42002-1540

Or phone: 502-442-8856.

OTHER MAQS EXHIBIT PUBLICATIONS

These books can be found in the MAQS bookshop and in local bookstores and quilt shops. If you are unable to locate a title in your area, you can order by mail from the publisher: AQS, P.O. Box 3290, Paducah, KY 42002-3290.

Please add $2 for the first book and $.40 for each additional one to cover postage and handling. International orders please add $2.50 for the first book and $1 for each additional one.

To order by VISA or MASTERCARD call: 1-800-626-5420 or fax: 1-502-898-8890.

Contemporary Quilts from The James Collection
Ardis James
#4525: AQS, 1995, 40 pages, 6" x 9", softbound, $12.95.

Gatherings: America's Quilt Heritage
Kathlyn F. Sullivan
#4526: AQS, 1995, 224 pages, 10" x 8½", softbound, $34.95.

Nancy Crow: Quilts and Influences
Nancy Crow
#1981: AQS, 1990, 256 pages, 9" x 12", hardcover, $29.95.

Nancy Crow: Work in Transition
Nancy Crow
#3331: AQS, 1992, 32 pages, 9" x 10", softbound, $12.95.

New Jersey Quilts – 1777 to 1950: Contributions to an American Tradition
The Heritage Quilt Project of New Jersey
#3332: AQS, 1992, 256 pages, 8½" x 11", softbound, $29.95.

Quilts: Old and New, A Similar View
Paul D. Pilgrim and Gerald E. Roy
#3715: AQS, 1993, 40 pages, 8¾" x 8", softbound, $12.95.

Quilts: The Permanent Collection – MAQS
#2257: AQS, 1991, 100 pages, 10" x 6½", softbound, $9.95.

Quilts: The Permanent Collection, Volume II – MAQS
#3793: AQS, 1994, 80 pages, 10" x 6½", softbound, $9.95.

The Log Cabin Returns to Kentucky: Quilts from the Pilgrim/Roy Collection
Paul D. Pilgrim and Gerald E. Roy
#3329: AQS, 1992, 36 pages, 9" x 7", softbound, $12.95.

Victorian Quilts, 1875–1900: They Aren't All Crazy
Paul D. Pilgrim and Gerald E. Roy
#3932: AQS, 1994, 64 pages, 6" x 9", softbound, $14.95.

Antique Quilts from The Miriam Tuska Collection
#4625: AQS, 1995, 40 pages, 6" x 9", softbound, $12.95.